SOWING SEEDS FOR THE SAVIOUR

CLAIRE ELIZABETH GROSE

Copyright © 2024 by Claire Elizabeth Grose

Compiled and edited by Michael Grose and June Kennedy

All rights reserved. No portion of this publication may be reproduced, stored in a retrieval system or transmitted in any form by any means – electronic, mechanical, photocopying, recording, or any other –except for brief quotation in printed reviews, without the prior written permission of the publisher.

Unless indicated otherwise, all scripture quotations in this book are from the following source:

The Good News Bible: The Bible in Today's English Version (TEV) © 1976 by the American Bible Society. Used with permission.

ISBN 978-0-6459888-1-9

Author contact information - clairegrose.heartmatters@gmail.com

Version 1.0

DEDICATION

This book is dedicated to Lindsay,
Father of our Children,
Pa to our Grandchildren and longtime friend.

CONTENTS

DEDICATION .... **IV**

CONTENTS .... **V**

PREFACE .... **VIII**

ACKNOWLEDGEMENTS .... **X**

   PART ONE 1
      MY DAILY PRAYER 4
      BEAUTIFUL BEYOND WORDS 5
      A BRAND NEW SEED 6
      BREAK OF DAY 7
      I'M IN YOUR HANDS LORD 8
      KNOW HEAVEN'S LOVE 9
      QUIET TIME TOGETHER 10
      DIVINE LOVE 11
      SEEDS OF LIGHT 14
      LOVING YOU 15
      TODAY'S BLESSINGS 16
      OVER AND OVER 17
      BIRTH DAY 18
      PASSING ON HIS LOVE 19
      LISTEN TO YOUR HEART 20
      MY LORD, MY GOD 21
      SOWING SEEDS 22
      LIFE IN YOU 23
      BLESS ME TODAY 26
      I'M WAITING ON YOU LORD 27
      MY ONLY COMPANY 28
      A CHRISTIAN HEART 29
   PART TWO 30
      SOWING SEEDS FOR THE SAVIOUR 33
      MY DEAREST 34
      ONE UNIT 35
      HAVING THE HEART OF GOD 36

SPIRITUAL WALKS *37*
WHEN YOU CALL MY NAME *38*
STEPPING STONES *41*
UP CLOSE AND PERSONAL WITH GOD *42*
THE GREAT HEALER *43*
THE HOURS OF TODAY *44*
THE YOU I KNOW *45*
WORDS OF COMFORT *46*
WONDERS OF YOUR LOVE *49*
YOU ARE WHERE I AM LORD *50*
BE STILL, BE QUIET *51*
YOU ARE ALL I EVER NEED *52*
WRAPPED IN THE ARMS OF JESUS *53*
MY LORD, MY LOVE *54*
ETERNAL SEEDS *57*
DON'T HURT YOURSELF ANYMORE *58*
I NEED YOU LORD *59*
A THANKFUL HEART *60*
A LOVE THAT DEEPENS *61*
IN THE ARMS OF THE SAVIOUR *62*
HE LIVES IN YOUR HOUSE *63*
HE CALLS FOR LOVE *64*
EVERY STEP OF THE WAY *65*
BECAUSE OF YOU LORD *66*
WALK CLOSER TO ME *67*
MOVING FORWARD *68*
PART THREE 69
WORK OF THE FAITHFUL *72*
SPIRIT LOVE *73*
THE GIFT OF LIFE *74*
THE POWER OF HIS WORD *75*
THE SWEETNESS OF YOUR LOVE *76*
SOVEREIGN LORD *77*
SEEDS OF CHANGE *80*
SACRED HOLY SPIRIT *81*

MOMENTS THAT SHINE	82
LISTEN TO HIS SPIRIT	83
KISS THE HAND OF RIGHTEOUSNESS	84
SPIRIT POWER	85
PART FOUR	86
HIS PIERCED HANDS	89
THE CALL OF THE CROSS	90
THE PRICE OF CALVARY	91
IN THE GARDEN WITH THE SAVIOUR	94
REDEMPTION	95
EXALT HIM	98
MIRACLE BIRTH	99
HOLY NIGHT CHRISTMAS EVE	100
CHRISTMAS BLESSINGS	101

PREFACE

Two things I just wanted to say about this book are, why I started writing and how I came by the title.

I grew up in the 1950's-1960's in Adelaide, South Australia, my life was pretty simple but wonderful. I was very lucky to have a secure family life, and my Mum and Dad brought the family up to treat others with respect, do the right thing, be courteous, and respect your elders. We had a strict upbringing and even as adults our parents never criticized us but encouraged us to do our best in life. They were "Aussie battlers" but we always managed to make it through the tough times!

They were people of integrity and cared about others and instilled that into our family.

Church was a big part of our lives growing up. We went to Sunday School at an early age and progressed up through the appropriate groups as we got older.

Youth groups, camps and church anniversaries were all important to the whole family. We competed in church sports teams, basketball and tennis with other parishes across Adelaide. Life-long friendships were in the making and cherished golden memories to look back on that would never fade.

Bible stories, hymns and choruses were all part of getting to know Jesus. This nurturing finally led me to the day Jesus came knocking on my heart's door. Being filled with the Holy Spirit is something I will never forget and the overwhelming power of His love that filled my whole being and propelled me to the front of the hall to give my heart to Him. No words can fully describe the joy I felt. That was in February 1968, I was 14 years of age. He has been my Shining Light ever since, and lives within me always.

So I thank my beautiful Mum and Dad for the way they raised me and for the foundation of knowing Jesus' love.

It was in His love that I started to write, in the autumn of 1993. My journey has brought me to this book "Sowing Seeds for the Saviour", my 11th book. In His Word He tells us to pass His message on and only with His help and in union with the Holy Spirit can we do this. "…God uses us to make the knowledge about Christ spread everywhere like a sweet fragrance." 2 Corinthians 2:14 Good News Bible. That brought the title to me.

He took our sin to The Cross, and replaced it with His forgiveness, which has given us eternal life, to all who believe that He died on the Cross at Calvary and three days later rose to life by His Heavenly Father who gave us the Holy Spirit. The Lord is now seated at the right hand of God in His heavenly Kingdom. What a revelation to rely on, knowing He is always ready to supply all our needs, to sow seeds to bring people to faith in Jesus.

When I was a young Christian reading my Bible was really important to me in getting to know Jesus as my personal Saviour and became the foundation that I built my faith on.

It gave me strength and courage as I began life in the workforce at the age of 16. Coming from a sheltered upbringing it was my lifeline to self-confidence and adapting to social life at work.
The poems reflect the everyday feelings and emotions that we feel as we meet the challenges of life and how the great magnitude of God's love can help us rise above them.

Many of these writings have been my first words of whispered prayer, so much that I have been moved to write them down at once and continue on in His wonderful and absolute love.

Together we write as He provides my inspiration.

All glory to Him, my precious Lord Jesus!

ACKNOWLEDGEMENTS

My heartfelt thanks to my beloved family, my Mum and Dad, Lilly and Ken, and my siblings Jeanette, June, Carol, Gloria and Lynne, for their never ending encouragement and support to me. To the rest of the family, you are all a precious link that joins us together.

To Michael and Andrew for your continual support to me in fulfilling my passion of writing poems for the Lord to help others through His Word.

A huge thank you to Junie for editing my poems and the coffees and lunches we enjoyed along the way.

To Joy Furnell for her Crown of Thorns drawing, you have an amazing gift, thank you Joy.

A special thank you to Salisbury Uniting Church, Adelaide for photos. Used by permission.

A big thank you to Carol, Dennis, Lynne, Karen, Jeff, Allan, and Barry for great photos.

To my friends and Church Families, thank you for your love and support.

To my beautiful sons, Michael and Andrew, and your families. Thank you for loving me, and I am so glad He gave you to me. I cherish my grandchildren, Ashleigh, Costa, Lailah and Jaxon. I love you all so much.

To you the reader, thank you for picking this book up and I pray you will find His peace and love on the pages ahead.

May He shower you all with His love and blessings.

PART ONE

"The man who reaps the harvest is being paid and gathers the crops for eternal life; so the man who plants and the man who reaps will be glad together."

John 4 : 36

SOWING SEEDS FOR THE SAVIOUR

A HARVEST OF BLESSINGS…
WILL COME YOUR WAY…

"…the seed is the word of God."

Luke 8 : 11

MY DAILY PRAYER

Be with me, stay with me,
Close by my side,
Fill me with your peace and love,
So my spirit shall surely fly
To the heights in your love,
As only you can give,
Prepare me for this day ahead,
So in me you'll always live.

BEAUTIFUL BEYOND WORDS

Holy Spirit You are
Beautiful beyond words,
A flame within me
That makes my heart yearn.

A love so faithful
Caring so much,
Soothing my soul
With Your tender touch.

Joy beyond compare
Permeates from You,
A presence unspeakable
My heart You renew.

A promise unshakeable
Will forever stay,
Because You are beautiful
And beyond words in every way.

My comfort, my guide
Who soothes and heals,
My love, my God
Who makes me want to kneel.

A BRAND NEW SEED

The Sun throws threads of gold
Across the open spaces,
Valleys, hills, lakes and streams
And many other places.

As she rises in the sky,
I love to watch Mother Nature,
Mile after mile passing by,
The Lord's perfect creation.

The wind runs a thousand fingers
Through the crops it's true,
Tossing the ears about,
Each one a seed brand new.

See the simple things of life
That come into view,
Just like each one of us,
We are a seed brand new.

BREAK OF DAY

Break of day, such a beautiful time,
As daylight thrills my heart,
Birds in song – an anthem!
For this fresh new start.

Yesterday now in the past,
As today breaks forth,
Whatever it brings I pray
"be with me today Lord."

Break of day so fresh,
The cool air will vitalize
My mind and body today
As I seize today's sunrise.

Thank You Lord for break of day,
As another page is turned
In the lives of many
For what today will serve.

I'M IN YOUR HANDS LORD

I'm in Your hands Lord,
Loving You adoring You,
My faith and trust so strong,
I know You'll guide me through.

I'm in Your hands Lord
Every day of my life,
I have no moment without You
Because You are by my side.

I'm in Your hands Lord,
You called me long ago
To be Your child,
Your blessings truly flow.

I'm in Your hands Lord
My Master, my everything,
Your glory shines within me,
I bow to You; my King!

KNOW HEAVEN'S LOVE

Call the Master to your side
So you will know His love,
Draw near to Him,
God's only dear Son.

Know Heaven's love
So pure, so rich, so divine,
Live it, love it, feel it,
So you can say, "He is mine."

He will change you on the inside,
Your heart will know humility,
A golden light will shine in you,
That truly sets you free.

Know Heaven's love
To reap His rewards,
No words can explain
"He couldn't love you more."

Know Heaven's love
So His Spirit can live in you,
Call Him into your heart,
Your life He will renew.

QUIET TIME TOGETHER

In this quiet time together,
I call You to my side,
In the faith and love I feel
That I just can't hide.

Your presence so real
Because my heart tells me so,
A blessing so rich
From You, I know.

My thoughts are hushed
As the joy I feel
Wraps my whole being
As in reverence I kneel.

My Holy Redeemer
Holds me in awe,
In this quiet time
Our love grows more and more.

The dawn so fresh,
Coolness is sweet,
This quiet time so real
As we two meet.

This reassurance awakes
A peace unspeakable,
In union with The Spirit
My heart is truly full.

DIVINE LOVE

Accept His invitation
To come into your heart,
It will take you to His mercy seat,
This is where your new life starts.

Knowing true divine love
Comes not from this life,
It is the nature of God
That can turn wrong to right.

It is by His Spirit
We receive divine love,
We can turn from our ways
When we open our heart to God.

He can mend the deepest hurt,
Change a tear to a smile,
He can wipe away a frown
And make a day worthwhile.

Divine love can change you
Like never before,
You will wear the mantle of God,
As you long to love Him more.

IN HIS NAME...
YOUR KINDNESS WILL PROSPER...

"So let us not become tired of doing good; for if we do not give up, the time will come when we will reap the harvest."

Galatians 6 : 9

SEEDS OF LIGHT

When I write Your Words Lord,
Seeds of light I sow,
I pray for a harvest
That will overflow.

Seeds of light will spread,
Shining on the heart
To the weary and worn,
They bring hope to their path.

Seeds of light are nourished
Deep in the Saviour's love,
Reflection of the Trinity
Redeemed through His blood.

Seeds of light will rise
And shine brightly on the earth,
Beacons so bright
In trust and faith we serve.

Seeds of light spread joy
Through His mercy and grace,
To the open heart so humble
Because they've seen His face.

Seeds of light stand together,
A radiance so bright,
Reflecting the light of God
Through His power and might.

LOVING YOU

Loving You is real Lord
To me as night and day,
You are forever with me,
In my heart You'll always stay.

Loving You is vital,
It can take so many years,
Sometimes it takes a lifetime
To break through doubts and fears.

Loving You refines me
Into the vessel I should be,
Your message I can share
So others can be free.

Loving You is easy
Because Your Spirit lives inside,
To fill my heart forever
With Your love that You provide.

TODAY'S BLESSINGS

Today's blessings will be many
When you place your trust in the Lord,
They will be wonderful
Whether they are big or small.

Put today in His hands
As the hours pass by,
Tell Him your cares
Share with Him day and night.

Today's blessings are real
Even when you don't recognize,
Something kind someone said
Will lift your spirit high.

Yes, today's blessings unknown
Until they arrive,
Be sure they will come
From the Saviour on high.

OVER AND OVER

Seeing Your sunset tonight
Brought pure joy to me,
Over and over Your love Lord
Is what I've seen.

Contentment and peace
Lays on my heart,
The beginning of evening
As daylight departs.

A thrill worth knowing
As my soul lights up,
This sunset remains
In my mind sure enough.

A sign that You Lord
Are in control,
As the sun comes to rest
And bows when it's told.

Your heavenlies displayed
Bring wonder and awe
To each heart that opens
To You more and more!

BIRTH DAY

Lord, this is the day You chose for me
To enter the world,
Nothing is by chance,
Your will is upheld.

This day is special
None other will do,
This day You chose for me,
To arrive that is true.

So, thank You precious Jesus
For the family You placed me in,
And my precious Mum who birthed me
Who one day I will see again.

Lord, You share each day with me,
My guiding shining light,
My Saviour and Lord forever,
I love You with all my might.

Yes, today is my birth day,
Only once a year,
You have already named
The ones I will hold dear.

PASSING ON HIS LOVE

The Lord may ask you to step
Outside your comfort zone today,
In obeying His commands
Your rewards will be arrayed.

He needs you to pass
His love along,
To where a need is great
Is where you belong.

We are His helpers
Of that you can be sure,
Passing on His love
Will bring His rewards.

It may be an errand
Or to change your plans today,
In passing on His love,
His will you have obeyed.

A small seed will be sown
By this kindly act,
In passing on His love,
Nothing will you lack.

LISTEN TO YOUR HEART

Listen to your heart
And how you feel,
The Holy Spirit will guide you
As you humbly kneel.

He will prompt you
To act accordingly,
When you listen to your heart
He will guide you tenderly.

Listen to your heart,
Ask for His wisdom to fall
Upon your soul,
Be open to His call.

Listen to your heart
Filled with the love of God,
He will steer your course
If Him, you lean upon.

MY LORD, MY GOD

My Lord and my God,
How I worship Thee,
Your Spirit so Holy
Abides with me.

My comfort, my guide
In all I do,
I only have to ask
For help from You.

My faith in You,
My love, so strong,
Forever with me
You do belong.

My Lord, my God,
Your blessings flow
Boundlessly to me,
That I surely know.

SOWING SEEDS

Spread His Word
Whenever you can,
Let His light shine
By lending a hand.

You may not realize
The good deeds you do,
By lending a hand
You are sowing seeds it's true.

The Saviour will work
On the smallest deed,
By lending a hand
You are sowing His seeds.

Just a thoughtful word
Or a smile will do,
Sow seeds for the Saviour
He wants you to.

When you live by the heart
That the Saviour owns,
You will spread many seeds
He will nurture to grow.

LIFE IN YOU

Precious Lord, I love
The life in You,
Ours for the taking
To make us brand new.

We have life in You
The eternal seed,
Through trust and faith
You supply our every need.

The life in You
Comes with power and strength,
The Holy Son of God,
Your Kingdom has no end.

Yes, life in You Lord
Is the only way,
All our tomorrows in Your glory
Your promise that's here to stay!

CELEBRATE HIS BEAUTY…
SUNRISE, SUNSET…

"May you always be joyful in your union with
the Lord. I say it again: rejoice!"

Philippians 4 : 4

BLESS ME TODAY

Bless me today with Your will,
While Your Spirit conveys to me
The fullness of Your love
As it opens for me to see.

For my path today
Help me journey as Your child,
May Your blessings come down
As You walk with me awhile.

Bless this day Lord,
In Your love divine,
My heart warms to You
As Your glory on me shines.

So, than You Lord
For Your blessings displayed
To my open heart
As You show me the way.

I'M WAITING ON YOU LORD

I'm waiting on You Lord,
Today has begun,
I'm waiting on You Lord
Because You are God's Son.

I'm waiting on You Lord,
The glorious King of Kings,
I'm waiting on You Lord,
I know You live within.

I'm waiting on You Lord,
My Shepherd and my Rock,
My Guide and my Shield,
Your care never stops.

I'm waiting on You Lord,
My companion day by day,
Take my hand, lead me on,
You will show me the way.

MY ONLY COMPANY

You are my only company Lord
All of the time,
You never leave me,
I'm so glad You are mine.

I can talk to you anytime
You never sleep,
You care for me constantly,
You hear every word I speak.

You take my cares and hurts,
They fade into Your light,
You replace them with Your balm,
So golden, so bright.

Your healing comforts me
More than I can say,
Through Your Holy Spirit
Who is with me night and day.

You are my only company Lord,
The lover of my soul,
Even when I don't realize,
Only You can make me whole.

A CHRISTIAN HEART

A Christian heart helps us rise
Above the challenges we meet,
Our trust and faith in Jesus
So surely sweet as sweet.

A Christian heart our teacher,
Keeps our thoughts in check,
Because the Lord of Righteousness
His standards He has set.

A Christian heart has battled
Storms and cloudy days,
But Jesus our shelter and refuge
Gives us hope along the way.

A Christian heart demands
Kind and thoughtful ways,
Restoring peace and calm
That we try to maintain.

A Christian heart reflects
A love that knows no end,
Sent by the Master Himself
Through His Spirit that He sends.

PART TWO

"Leave all your worries with him, because he cares for you."

1 Peter 5 : 7

COMPASSION ATTRACTS...
THE APPLAUSE OF HEAVEN...

"Help carry one another's burdens, and in this way you will obey the law of Christ."

Galatians 6 : 2

SOWING SEEDS FOR THE SAVIOUR

Sowing seeds for the Saviour
Means a friendly word or two,
To give a helping hand
Will echo through and through.

The faintest word is heard
In the realms of His home,
The wonder of the heavenlies
Includes His glorious Throne.

A moment of your time
Can save a wounded soul,
When they see your peace and calm
It's His Spirit that makes you whole.

Sowing seeds for the Saviour
Is work beyond compare,
He sees your caring heart
And has rewards that He will share.

Sowing seeds for the Saviour
Is work you just can't hide,
Because in knowing Him
Your seeds will multiply.

MY DEAREST

My dearest precious Lord,
The love You placed in me,
Can only be from Heaven
Because it came from Thee.

Messiah of the world,
My dearest King of Kings,
You came quietly in a stable
To save mankind from sin.

My dearest Prince of Peace,
Prophesied in Your Word
That a Saviour would come
To the world to serve.

My dearest Counsellor
I can tell You my cares,
You console me tenderly
Because faith in You I bear.

My dearest Almighty God,
Heaven's light and love,
I call you into my heart
Because You are God's only Son.

ONE UNIT

God's family; one unit,
United by the Cross
That He took for one and all,
Love Him we must.

As one unit we are linked
In His never ending love,
Forever within us,
His family we become.

As His sons and daughters,
We are nurtured in His care
We can show His love to others
Because His Cross we bear.

As one unit we belong,
Sisters and brothers we all share
God's love and mercy
For we are in His care!

HAVING THE HEART OF GOD

How lucky we are to know
People with the heart of God,
One in His family
Who share divine love.

Having the heart of God
Means being caring and kind,
Thoughtful and not proud,
The freedom to say, "He is mine".

An unspoken bond
Joins us to be one,
We may not know each other
But we are children of the Son.

We share almighty love,
We received His mercy and grace,
We are privileged to wear His name
Because His Spirit showed us faith.

Having the heart of God
Is a baptism of the soul,
Owned by His Spirit,
Who now has made us whole.

SPIRITUAL WALKS

I pray that your spiritual walk
Will deepen in the Father's love
Filled with the joys and wonders
From His heaven above.

May His mercy and grace
Overflow in your heart,
May it know the many blessings
That only He can impart.

His knowledge and wisdom
Will be made clear
As you journey along
With the One so Dear.

May your spiritual walk deepen
In Jesus Christ the Lord,
As your love grows
Because He couldn't love you more!

WHEN YOU CALL MY NAME

When You call my name Lord
I know I belong to You,
The connection so strong,
A bond from me to You.

When You call my name Lord,
I feel I've come home,
You, my heavenly Father
Your love to me You've shown.

When You call my name Lord,
My soul turns to You,
My heart receives Your joy
That makes me feel brand new.

When You call my name Lord
From Your Throne above,
I pray heaven's angels are singing
In Your glory full of love.

BEING GENEROUS…
WILL BRING GOD'S FAVOUR…

"…I will make all my splendour pass before you and in your presence I will pronounce my sacred name."

Exodus 33 : 19

STEPPING STONES

The stepping stones of life
Can take us anywhere,
Steeped in trust
Because we are in Your care.

Sometimes they are missing
That's when we rely on trust,
Using our faith in the Saviour
We can leap over the shadows to come.

The stepping stones of life
Can bruise or hurt our feet,
But the balm of the Saviour
Will heal so complete.

They may lay upon steep mountains
Or tracks on grassy fields,
But living in trust and faith
Our path You will reveal.

The stepping stones of life
We can choose to take or leave,
They can lead you to victory
If in Jesus, you will believe.

UP CLOSE AND PERSONAL WITH GOD

Up close and personal with God
Is where He wants us to be,
My soul overflows
With His love for me.

His love is so passionate,
I must pass it on
That's why I write
Because for you, He longs.

His message is known
Through the centuries of time,
How He endured Calvary
To give us eternal life.

I share each day
With my precious Lord,
Every care I give to Him
Because it's Him I adore.

Yes, up close and personal
With God indeed,
Your soul will rejoice
Because of the Holy Trinity.

THE GREAT HEALER

You are the great healer Lord
In all sorrows in our lives,
For You are love itself Lord
Strength You will provide.

Broken hearts You mend,
Wounds and scars You soothe,
Doubts and fears You take
But Your love we will never lose.

You are the great healer Lord
To all who will repent
And ask for Your forgiveness
That every day You send.

So I pray that the world will listen
For Your voice that sounded long ago,
It's still the same today,
The Great Healer, who I know.

THE HOURS OF TODAY

Walking through the hours of today
Help is at hand,
Jesus is closer than you think,
He truly understands.

He wants to celebrate your joys
And lift you out of your sorrows
When you share with Him
All of your tomorrows.

Walking through the hours of today,
Whether slow or fast,
The Saviour will gently guide you,
All you need to do is ask.

He craves to be your guide
Every step of the way,
Simply ask Him for help
Just for today.

Moving through the hours of today
A task it need not be,
Look to the heavenlies for comfort
He will supply all your needs.

THE YOU I KNOW

Lord, I want to see Your beauty
And the You I know,
To always feel You close
Because I love You so.

The You I know
And the calm I feel
When my heart is settled,
Your magnitude revealed.

The richness of Your Spirit,
The healing and love You send
Your wonder and awe awaken,
My fragility You mend.

Yes, the You I know Lord,
Forever surreal;
Always around me,
Love You? I always will!

The You I know Lord
Is with me every day,
I am never alone,
You are in my heart to stay.

WORDS OF COMFORT

Words of comfort from the Saviour
Bring peace and calm to me,
When I feel the threat of fear
His Words I seek to read.

His written Word is a lifeline
When hope seems a long way off,
But reading His Words of love
Is a supply that will never stop.

When shadows fall around me
And the sun just doesn't seem to shine,
I can't give in to the darkness,
I call for Jesus, the living vine.

Yes, His Words of comfort are fervent,
Bringing life, light and strength
To my heart that keeps on wanting
His love that has no end.

ENCOURAGEMENT...
WARMS THE HEART...

"And so encourage one another and help one another, just as you now are doing."

1 Thessalonians 5 : 11

WONDERS OF YOUR LOVE

The wonders of Your love Lord
Go beyond words,
A feeling unspeakable
Makes my heart yearn.

Your wonders made in heaven,
Sent to us below
Can leave us in awe,
Your beauty on show.

The wonders of Your love Lord
Can mend a shattered heart
And the deepest hurts and wounds
That have left a mark.

The wonders of Your love Lord,
The Holy Spirit sends,
Into the soul forever
From Your world without end.

YOU ARE WHERE I AM LORD

You are where I am Lord
Though my circumstances may change,
You are there for me Lord
Your Spirit remains the same.

Change is never easy
Settling in takes a while,
But You are where I am Lord,
In Your place and time.

Wherever I go You are with me Lord,
My focus needs to be on You
Because You are where I am Lord
You will walk me through.

Your power never changes
Your love spreads more and more,
Your Spirit so overwhelming
You love me to the core.

You are where I am Lord,
At home or at work,
You will never desert me
Because You loved me first.

BE STILL, BE QUIET

I must be still and quiet
So I can hear Your voice,
Then I can claim Your calm
To still the noise.

Your tender grace soothes me
From the daily toils I know,
But You supply my needs
Through Your mercy that flows.

I must be still, be quiet
So those inner voices can cease,
Then I will hear Your tender Words
That bring me to my knees.

Yes, in the quietness Lord
I can hear You speak,
Then I can focus on You
When we come to meet.

YOU ARE ALL I EVER NEED

My companion always
For love and peace
I only have to ask
In faith to receive.

Only You can erase
The sorrows of my life,
By Your grace and mercy
Through faith You will provide.

You are my all
Every day of my life,
My fortress, my stronghold,
My true shining light.

Your precious Holy Spirit
Shows You to me,
In wonder and awe,
You're all I ever need.

WRAPPED IN THE ARMS OF JESUS

I'm wrapped in the arms of Jesus,
In surrender I come to You,
Filled to the brim in Your love
That sweetly flows from You.

Wrapped in the arms of Jesus,
No safer place to be,
Secure in His love
That brings Eternity.

I'm wrapped in the arms of Jesus
Who has changed my life so much,
As I look back over the years
I see His gentle touch.

Wrapped in the arms of Jesus,
My lifeline and my guide,
My tomorrows I leave in Your hands
Because in me You abide.

MY LORD, MY LOVE

My Lord, my love,
I need You tonight
To hush the fears
I feel inside.

Soothe me and calm me,
Let Your peace again reign,
In my own strength I can't
But in You I can change.

My Lord, my love
I must keep my gaze on You,
Help me to rise above
To the strength in You.

My Lord, my love,
One thing is clear,
Our love will keep me drawn
To Your side so near.

HE'S THRILLED WITH YOUR VICTORY…
A KIND WORD YOU SHARED…

"he will make your righteousness shine
like the noonday sun."

Psalm 37 : 6

ETERNAL SEEDS

The Lord calls us to sow
Eternal seeds when we can,
To be a living witness
And care for our fellow man.

Eternal seeds are found
In many ways you know,
Shown by the way you act
When you talk seeds can be sown.

God's grace and mercy
Will show in your heart,
Prompting you to serve Him
By helping others on your path.

Eternal seeds are precious,
They will grow like the reaching vine,
Fed by the Saviour's love
Where they will flourish in ageless time.

DON'T HURT YOURSELF ANYMORE

Don't hurt yourself anymore
From the actions of others,
Stay close to the Saviour
And the peace He offers.

Ask for His peace and calm
To see you through the day,
Be sure His Holy Spirit
Will comfort you today.

Focus on the wonders
And beauty you have seen,
Your successful challenges
That brought you victory.

In the Saviour's Name
You can succeed,
Don't hurt yourself anymore,
His glory you will see.

I NEED YOU LORD

I need You Lord beside me
In every passing day,
Let Your presence be fervent
Every step of the way.

I need You Lord this moment,
My precious Heavenly Host,
To hush the fears inside me,
For Your arms to cradle me close.

I need You every day Lord,
My companion and my shield,
So I can tell You everything,
On You my trust I'll build.

Without You I am nothing,
My strength relies on You,
Powered by Your Spirit
I can do all things through You.

A THANKFUL HEART

A thankful heart from answered prayer
When the journey has been long,
Trust and faith a necessity
In the Saviour can make you strong.

A thankful heart is a happy heart,
Seated deep in the Master's love,
In praise you can thank the Father
For sending His Spirit to us.

A thankful heart is a thoughtful heart,
Inspired by The Spirit,
A message to the soul
To all who will hear it.

A thankful heart knows mercy
Abundant and true,
Full of overflowing grace
From the Master who made you.

A thankful heart is a patient heart
That waits on the Lord,
No rush; all is well,
His angels will applaud!

A LOVE THAT DEEPENS

Only the love of Christ,
So sacred and divine,
Can deepen in your heart
When He says, "you are mine."

He promised to never leave you,
To always be by your side,
Eternity is His gift
When your heart opens wide.

Only His love can deepen,
It's a love that knows no bounds,
Showered with wonders and awe
In Jesus alone is found.

He longs to show you his realm
And the joy that awaits
But as your love deepens
You will know through your faith.

A love that deepens,
Can only be from the Lord Jesus Christ,
So pure and eternal
Will change the way you feel inside!

IN THE ARMS OF THE SAVIOUR

In the arms of the Saviour,
His glory will reign,
His golden light will shine
To show you the way.

Your open heart will receive
His blessings untold,
When you're in the arms of the Saviour
Your destiny will unfold.

Your obedience will bring
His rewards to you,
That He longs to give out
Because His promise is true.

In the arms of the Saviour
His teachings will be revealed,
So your open heart
He will surely over fill.

HE LIVES IN YOUR HOUSE

He lives in your house
And hears what you say,
He knows everything about you
And still loves you anyway.

He lives in your house,
He cares for you so much,
His heart aches for those
Who haven't accepted His love.

He can take your hurts,
With one touch they are gone,
He'll wipe your tears away
When they fall every time.

He'll rejoice with you when you're happy,
He'll turn a frown into a smile,
He never leaves your side,
He'll walk with you every mile.

Yes, He lives in your house every day,
He craves your invitation and love,
Open your heart to the Saviour
So you will have a place in His home above.

HE CALLS FOR LOVE

The Lord calls for a love
Humble and pure,
One that forgives
Is steadfast and sure.

His love withstands our failures,
He sees our worst and our shame,
But through His grace and mercy
We are forgiven in His Name.

He calls for love,
His message is still the same,
He longs for our acceptance
As we pray in His Name.

He calls for love,
In all we do,
Through His Holy Spirit
He will reveal it to you.

EVERY STEP OF THE WAY

Every step of the way
I trust You Lord,
From morning 'til night
I love you even more.

Every step of the way
My future unknown,
I trust You Lord
My life's seeds already sown.

Every step of the way,
Challenges may rise
But I trust You Lord
Remind me I'm Your child!

Every step of the way
I trust You Lord,
When I'm tempted to doubt,
On my faith I will draw.

Every step of the way
I trust You Lord,
Your choices for me made long ago
Before I was born!

BECAUSE OF YOU LORD

Because of You Lord
I can survive
The topsy turvy days of life
As they pass me by.

Because of You Lord
I can smile again,
Though the challenges I face
Your strength You send.

Because of You Lord
And Your care of me,
I can endure this life
Because of Thee.

Because of You Lord
My heart has changed,
The Holy Spirit came to me,
In Your Name I am saved.

Yes Lord, because of You
I am free,
The greatest gift You gave me
Was surely Calvary!

WALK CLOSER TO ME

Walk closer to me Dear One
So the shadows of life will disappear,
Guard me with Your Spirit
Who takes away my fears.

Walk closer to me Dear One
So I don't feel alone,
May we walk in unison
Towards Your heavenly Throne.

Walk closer to me Dear One
So my steps lighter will be,
Along my journey of life
I feel safe when You walk with me.

Walk closer to me Dear One
So I can see Your heavenly smile,
As Your arms draw me close
To rest on Your breast awhile.

Walk closer to me Lord
So a peace and calm I can feel,
Within my soul forever
Because to me You are so real.

MOVING FORWARD

We're moving forward
With You by our side,
Memories of yesterday
In time will subside.

Whether they made you smile
Or brought a shadow to your world,
Moving forward is the key
So you can be upheld.

With faith and trust release them
For healing to take place,
The Lord will be beside you,
He will meet you face to face.

Yes, moving forward is the key
To hope in His Light,
His awe and wonder will change you
Because you are precious in His sight.

PART THREE

"…Strive for righteousness, godliness, faith, love, endurance, and gentleness. Run your best in the race of faith, and win eternal life for yourself; …"

1 Timothy 6 : 11 - 12

THE JOY OF THE HOLY SPIRIT…
WILL MAKE YOUR HEART SHINE…

"And to all these qualities add love, which binds all things together in perfect unity."

Colossians 3 : 14

WORK OF THE FAITHFUL

The work of the faithful
Is to spread the Saviour's love
Because that's what He is
In His realm above.

The faithful called by God
Through His Spirit here,
Prepares us for Eternity,
Each one He holds so dear.

The work of the faithful
Is to spread many seeds
To help at any time
With hope from caring deeds.

The work of the faithful
With humble empathy,
Shows the standard of the King
To help those in need.

The work of the faithful
Is to honour His Word,
Carrying His name a privilege,
His beloved we must serve.

SPIRIT LOVE

Spirit love from the Saviour
Is joy beyond compare,
The heart warms
When you speak of Him there.

A complete feeling
So rich in Spirit love,
It knows no bounds or limits
Such ecstasy from above.

A sure-footed foundation
In the Saviour's love
Will equip you always
For the challenges that come.

Spirit love so tender
As gentle as the breeze,
Sweet as perfumed roses
All made by Thee.

Spirit love overwhelms,
When He calls your heart will know,
An invitation you must answer
Because He loves you so.

THE GIFT OF LIFE

The gift of life so precious,
We can call it as it is,
Our choices make a difference
To the way we live.

The gift of life so overwhelming
When a baby is born,
Little soul pure in heart and spirit
That God alone has formed.

The gift of life from the Saviour,
A priceless sacrifice,
Echoes through the ages,
His gift of eternal life.

The gift of life is a promise
From Jesus Christ our Lord,
We can pass to Eternity
When we claim Him Lord of Lords.

THE POWER OF HIS WORD

The power of Your Word Lord
Can heal a broken heart,
Give strength in need,
Be the light in the dark.

The power of Your Word Lord
Is a balm so complete,
It will soothe and heal the wounds
That always seem so deep.

You come in calm and peace
To those who call You near,
They will receive Your grace and mercy
Because to You they are so dear.

Whoever believes the power of Your Word
Will have a place by Your side,
In faith they are made new again
You will love them for all time.

The power of Your Word Lord
Will reveal the heavenlies,
When You return with great glory,
We will know rhapsody!

THE SWEETNESS OF YOUR LOVE

The sweetness of Your love Lord
Is ever true,
No words can describe
This gift that comes from You.

Sweeter than a fragrance
From an expensive perfume,
Lasting longer than life,
Eternal are You.

The sweetness of Your love Lord
Like gentle ripples to the shore
Will reach out forever
To love us even more.

The sweetness of Your love Lord
Can forgive the darkest sin,
A star that shines in You
Will brighten one's heart within.

The sweetness of Your love Lord,
No gift on earth can compare,
Heaven's wonder and glory
Are waiting for us there.

SOVEREIGN LORD

Sovereign Lord, my Jesus,
Son of Almighty God,
I claim You as my Saviour,
You I can lean upon.

I've never known precious Lord
Such divine love as this,
Your Holy Spirit came to me
And showed me Heaven's bliss.

So overwhelming;
The power of Your love,
Such truth and life changing
Shown from You above.

So dear Lord Jesus
Stay with me today,
I need You every second,
Your sovereignty displayed.

YOUR THOUGHTFULNESS...
WILL MULTIPLY...

"...how rich are the wonderful blessings he promises his people, and how very great is his power at work in us who believe..."

Ephesians 1 : 18 - 19

SEEDS OF CHANGE

The world spins in the universe
Made by His Holy Hand,
Our names are written in His "Book Of Life"
For the believers of The Lamb.

He placed Sun and Moon
In their lofty place,
To give warmth and rest
As Earth revolves in Space.

From the beginning to the end
We are a seed of change,
All things will be made new again
When we turn the final page.

He put in place His Seasons
To dress His Earth in wealth,
He made Mother Nature
To make her presence felt.

We are seeds of change
Made in the image of the King,
Our spirit will open like a flower
When our final song we sing.

SACRED HOLY SPIRIT

Beautiful You; sacred and holy
From the Saviour a gift
Who heals and comforts
When He lives within.

Beyond words to tell
How glorious You are,
Great protector and guide
You came from beyond the stars.

The Lord gave You to us
To abide in the Christian heart,
To remind us of His love
And how the two will never part.

My light, my love
To lead me on,
Through sadness and joy
You make me strong.

Precious You; Holy Spirit
No words enough to describe,
So sacred, so Holy
You shroud me in Your light.

MOMENTS THAT SHINE

Moments that shine in your heart
Are when His Spirit calls to you,
An anointing so overwhelming
That completely embraces you.

A union you feel
With the Spirit from the Lord,
He can call at anytime
Because it's you He adores.

A message so strong,
You just can't ignore,
When He stirs the heart
You surely feel restored.

His Holy Spirit brings
Moments that shine
Because in you He lives,
He longs to call you "mine".

LISTEN TO HIS SPIRIT

It's easy to give in
To the challenges of life,
But listen to His Spirit
Who can change the wrong to right.

His message is simple,
Ask for His guiding hand,
He will honour your request
When you listen to His commands.

Though the world tells you different,
It's full of me, me, me,
But the Saviour calls for mercy
That you'll know when you believe.

It's through faith you can win
When your heart tells you so,
Listen to His Spirit
Because He loves you so!

KISS THE HAND OF RIGHTEOUSNESS

The Light of the world,
The one true vine
Kiss the hand of righteousness,
The hand of the Divine.

Kiss the hand of righteousness
That heals all open wounds
With a balm from only heaven
That can heal and soothe.

It's a love to last forever
That truly is sublime,
Kiss the hand of righteousness
That reaches for mankind.

With palms that bear the marks
A symbol of sacrifice and truth,
Kiss the hand of righteousness
Of his sacrifice for you.

Kiss the hand of righteousness
That holds a golden crown,
Waiting for you in heaven
Where the Saviour can be found.

SPIRIT POWER

Spirit power will touch
The deepest part of your soul,
The home He has made
In you to make you whole.

Spirit power will heal
The widest, deepest wound,
It comes with His anointing
To heal and to soothe.

Spirit power will warm
The coldest, lonely heart,
That knows winter's chill,
And scars that left their mark.

Spirit power so mighty,
Reveals eternal love
From the Lord God Himself
That will last into the age to come!

PART FOUR

"It was about twelve o'clock when the sun stopped shining and darkness covered the whole country until three o'clock; and the curtain hanging in the Temple was torn in two."

Luke 23 : 44 - 45

JESUS DIED FOR OUR SIN...
SO WE COULD HAVE ETERNAL LIFE...

"Jesus cried out in a loud voice
"Father! In your hands I place my spirit!"
He said this and died."

Luke 23 : 46

HIS PIERCED HANDS

The hands of God so glorious,
No words can justify,
The power and strength that yields
Miracles for you and I.

His pierced hands stretched forth
To reach for hurting souls,
To save them from their pain
That prevents them feeling whole.

His pierced hands can heal
The deepest wound that weeps,
Causing tears to run so free,
Now Jesus, your heart will seek.

His pierced hands so precious
Bore the nails of Calvary,
Will forever want to hold you
In His home for eternity.

Knowing Him as your Saviour
Battles you will win,
When you talk to His Spirit,
His Light will shine within!

THE CALL OF THE CROSS

The call of the Cross
Ignites my love,
For the murmurs of Easter
And the sacrifice to come

In faultless love
He gave His all
To save mankind
That was the Father's call.

His sight was on Heaven
And the joy to come,
Reunited with His Father
In their glorious love.

One price for all
That bought eternal life,
With the King of Glory
Forever by His side.

Yes, the call of the Cross,
Eternal it will be,
His sacrifice given
To set us free.

THE PRICE OF CALVARY

The price of Calvary
No man can ever pay,
It's treasure is priceless
It is paid for always.

Jesus Christ our Saviour
Came to earth for this cause,
Sent by His Father
To be our Redeemer; our Lord.

He stood before a crowd
Who chose a thief to be freed,
The son of Man stood quietly
And was sentenced to Calvary.

The Son of God is pure,
No sin to be found
But He carried a heavy Cross
On a track of stoney ground.

He kept His sight on Heaven
And our eternal gift He gave,
The price of Calvary
We can never repay!

JESUS IS ALIVE…
HEAVEN ROARS…

"Go throughout the whole world and preach the gospel to all mankind. Whoever believes and is baptized will be saved……After the Lord Jesus had talked with them, he was taken up to heaven and sat at the right side of God."

Mark 16 : 15 - 16, 19

IN THE GARDEN WITH THE SAVIOUR

In the garden with the Saviour,
His sacrifice complete,
The freshness of the morning,
His presence fragrant sweet.

Angels came to proclaim
The Lord had been raised,
Only the torn strips of cloth
Revealed where His body had laid.

His triumph over death
In His Word was prophesied,
Victory now acclaimed
"On the third day He will rise."

Glory in the garden,
None sweeter to find,
Mary thought He was a gardener
But it truly was the Lord Divine.

In the garden with the Saviour,
The agony overcome,
Now rapture and joy remain
With God's own precious Son.

He carried the Cross for us
So we can live in Eternity,
Forever by His side,
We too can claim victory!

REDEMPTION

A never-ending redemption
From Jesus Christ our Lord,
Is ours when we accept Him
To be our Saviour and more.

His power and grace
Will fill you to the brim,
When you commit to love Him
Then His Spirit lives within.

His never-ending redemption
Is for all time,
Your sins were forgiven
From that day on the Cross, He died.

Confess with your heart
That He is the Risen Lord,
His Father raised Him from the grave
Now redemption is yours!

Believe in your heart,
Confess with your lips,
Redemption is yours,
Now you belong to Him!

ETERNAL JOY...
THE FIRST HOLY NIGHT...

"The angel said to her, "Don't be afraid, Mary; God has been gracious to you. You will become pregnant and give birth to a son, and you will name him Jesus. He will be great and will be called the Son of the Most High God...""

Luke 1 : 30 - 32

EXALT HIM

Exalt His Holy Name,
"Jesus" He shall be called,
An angel appeared to Mary
To reveal God's Holy call.

A blessing through and through
Joseph took Mary for his wife,
She gave birth to the Saviour
On that Holy Night.

Glory beamed from the stable,
Overhead the Star shone bright,
The Baby Messiah lay in the Manger,
It was Christmas Night.

Exalt His Holy Name,
The name above all names,
Immanuel, The Saviour,
Born this very day.

Hallelujah, Hallelujah,
Christ has come to save,
The Saviour, our Eternal Father,
Our Redeemer lives today.

MIRACLE BIRTH

As prophesied centuries before,
Mary would bear the Prince of Peace,
The miracle birth of the Saviour
Will bring all people to their knees.

Conceived by the Holy Spirit,
God chose this gentle soul
To birth His Only Son,
To bring salvation we are told.

His Holy Word proclaims
His miracle birth to the world,
He will be called "Immanuel",
His message we must tell.

The miracle birth of the Saviour
Remains from age to age,
His message lives forever,
Eternal Life He proclaimed.

In Bethlehem, a humble stable,
His miracle birth took place,
He came for this one purpose,
For the world, He came to save.

HOLY NIGHT CHRISTMAS EVE

It was Christmas Eve,
Angels sang with pure delight,
The Saviour was born
This very night.

In a humble stable
Shepherds found the Babe
Wrapped in swaddling clothes,
They worshipped Him, amazed.

This Holy Night, Christmas Eve
So deep and still,
Magi travelled from afar
To adore and lowly kneel.

Precious gifts they brought to Him,
Frankincense, Myrrh and Gold,
Lovingly carried from afar,
The newborn King to behold.

Holy Night, Christmas Eve
Will forever remain,
Two thousand years forward
We still worship His Name.

CHRISTMAS BLESSINGS

Christmas blessings fill my heart,
The joy is so profound,
The birth of the Saviour
From Heaven coming down.

Christmas blessings shower
Goodwill to all mankind,
The message from the angels
Of the Messiah we can find.

Christmas blessings abound
In hearts who love the King,
Wonders of His birth
And eternal life He brings.

Christmas blessings last all year
Through the Saviour's love He sends,
Every day for His beloved
That is forever without end.

ALSO BY CLAIRE GROSE

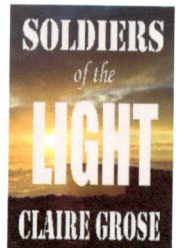
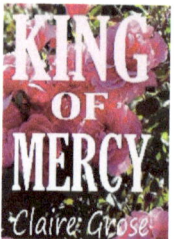

ABOUT THE AUTHOR

Claire worked as a Government Public Servant in the Lands Department, Adelaide, South Australia until she married and became a mother of two boys.

She later returned to the work force during which time she gained a "Living Hope" Phone Counselling certificate which influenced her need to help others.

Through this and personal experience she found herself inspired by God's love to put pen to paper.

PHOTO CREDITS

COVER PHOTO: Wheat Crop; S.A. Claire Grose

Page 2: Climbing Rose; S.A. – Karen and Jeff
Page 12: Stag Horn Plant; Qld. – Carol and Dennis
Page 24: Witta Sunset; Qld – Carol and Dennis
Page 31: Bromeliaceae Plant; Qld. – Carol and Dennis
Page 39: Croton Plant; NSW. – Allan and Barry
Page 47: Bismarck Palm; NSW. – Allan and Barry
Page 55: Aeonium Flowers; S.A. – Lynne
Page 70: Mt Tibrogargan; Qld. – Claire Grose
Page 78: Gardners Falls; Qld. – Carol and Dennis
Page 87: Olive Grove; S.A. – Claire Grose
Page 92: Salisbury Uniting Church Cross; S.A. – Claire Grose
Page 96: Salisbury Uniting Church Candles; S.A. – Claire Grose

SOWING SEEDS FOR THE SAVIOUR

www.ingramcontent.com/pod-product-compliance
Lightning Source LLC
Chambersburg PA
CBHW042043290426
44109CB00001B/16